AF572042

compiled by
Penrose Colyer
German by Ruth Jahnke

illustrations by
Colin Mier
and Wendy Lewis

I Can Read GERMAN

My First English~German Word Book

Contents

ISBN 0 85654 026 9

Printed in Italy by New Interlitho SpA

Reading German

In Germany you read German wherever you go – and without looking at a single book. There are names of German shops, such as *Lebensmittel* (grocer's), *Schlachter* (butcher's), and *Supermarkt* (supermarket); signposts such as *Berlin 100* (100 kilometres), and advertisements for German things. In order to get around and know what to do you have to be able to read signs such as *U-Bahn* (underground railway), *Nichtraucher* (no smoking), *Bitte nicht aus dem Fenster lehnen* (do not lean out of the window), *Ausgang* (exit), *Fahrkarten-Schalter* (ticket office) and many others.

So when you go to Germany, as you probably will one day, it is important that you should be able to read German. And even if you never go to Germany you can read German books and magazines which can be bought in your own country.

With this book you practise reading German. If you are learning it at school, you will probably know some of the words already; and you will learn some new ones, too. Many of the words appear again and again, so that by the time you get to the end of the book you will know them well.

Talking German

Talking German means not only saying German words but also making German sounds. Some of the sounds of German are the same as English ones; but some are completely different, and the only way to be able to say them correctly is by listening hard to a German-speaking person and looking at him at the same time. If you watch carefully, you will see that his mouth often makes different shapes from those made by someone talking English.

German sounds are much sharper and often shorter than English ones. You must speak each word very clearly. To produce these sharper sounds, flex the muscles of your mouth and move your lips more than you would do when speaking English. Let us try one example: *Zigeuner* (gypsy) is pronounced "Tseegoyna". For saying "Zi-" your mouth must take the shape of a wide grin. For "-eu" your lips are rounded and close together, while for "-ner" they are half open. Try to say this word and make your mouth take these various forms.

The vowels

In German as in English the vowels are the letters a, e, i, o and u. Listen carefully to the vowels in English words like "b*a*by" or "st*o*ve". You will find that for the one letter you make in fact two sounds: "a-e" and "o-u". In German however, vowels are always pure, unless we have two vowels together as in "H*au*s" (house). This word sounds exactly like the English one.

Finally, there are some letters which are not found in English words. The vowels a, o, u are sometimes written with two dots: ä, ö, ü. These dots make the vowels sound lighter. There is also a strange looking letter called "eszet": ß. It is spoken like the sharp s in "house".

Punctuation

The same punctuation marks are used as in English, but quotation marks are usually written in a different position, e.g. „Was ist das?" All nouns, not just proper names, begin with a capital letter.

The following words, which all appear in the book, contain many of the German sounds that are different from those you use in English. With each word there is a guide to how to say it. If you can say these words correctly, you will be beginning to talk German.

Mann: man
a: short, as in English "to come"

wäh-len: to choose
ä: long, as in English "where?", *w*: must always be spoken like the English *v*

kau-fen: to buy
au: as in English "house"

Fräulein: miss
äu: as in English "boy", *ei*: as in English "mine"

Freund: friend
eu: as in English "boy"
(*äu* and *eu* are spoken exactly the same way), *d*: at the end of a word it sounds like *t*.

Meer: sea
ee: long, a sound halfway between "h*e*re" and "h*ai*r".

wie viele?: how many?
ie: long, as in English "kn*ee*", *v*: is usually pronounced like an English *f*, (though sometimes like an English *v*).

schwim-men: to swim
i: as in English "to sw*i*m", *sch*: the same sound as the English *sh*.

Zoo: zoo
z: must be pronounced like *ts*, *oo*: long, as in English "st*o*ve" but without the tinge of *u*.

Roll-trep-pe: escalator
o: short, as in English "b*o*nfire", *e*: similar to *a* in English "m*a*p", but shorter.

jung: young
u: as in English "b*u*tcher", *j*: is always spoken like *y* in "*y*oung".

Kü-che: kitchen
ü: start by saying *i*, then push your mouth forward as if you wanted to whistle, *ch*: very soft, as in the English name "*H*ugh".

möchte: would like
ö: rather like *e* in "to *e*rr", *ch*: soft as in "Küche".

Schlach-ter: butcher
a: as in "Mann", *ch*: as in the Scottish word "Lo*ch*". (After *a*, *o*, *u*, *au* one must speak *ch* the "Scottish" way, in all other cases it is soft.)

Sylvia
y: must be pronounced here like *ü* in "Küche" (but sometimes it sounds like the English *y*), *v*: sounds here like the English *v*.

Fuß-ball-spiel: (football)
u: as in English "z*oo*", ß: sharp *s* as in "hou*s*e", *sp*: sounds like *shp*

Perhaps this all sounds somewhat complicated, but understanding what people mean is not always as complicated as you might expect. When you listen to a German-speaking person, do not try to pick out every word that is said. Try instead to get an idea of the sort of sounds that are made. Try also to tell what a whole sentence sounds like. Remember that a person uses gestures and facial expressions as well as words to convey the meaning. These gestures and expressions will help you to understand that meaning. It is important to hear and watch as many German-speaking people as possible, (in person or on the television or at the movies). Listening to the radio and records can also help you a lot.

Wie viele?
How many?

Vier Flaschen Coca-Cola
Four bottles of Coca-Cola

Magst du Coca-Cola?
Do you like Coca-Cola?

Sechs Regenschirme
Six umbrellas

Wie viele Regentropfen sind es?
How many raindrops are there?

Drei Giraffen
Three giraffes

Wie viele Augen haben sie?
How many eyes have they?

Und wie viele Flecken?
And how many spots?

Einhundert?
A hundred?

Zwei große Drachen
Two large dragons

Eine Insel
One island

Wie viele Menschen sind auf dieser Insel?
How many people are there on the island?

Kerzen
Candles

Jemand hat Geburtstag.
It's somebody's birthday.

Er ist neun Jahre alt.
He is nine.

Zehn Goldfische
Ten goldfish

Fünf glückbringende Hufeisen
Five lucky horseshoes

Hat dieser Mann Glück?
Is this man lucky?

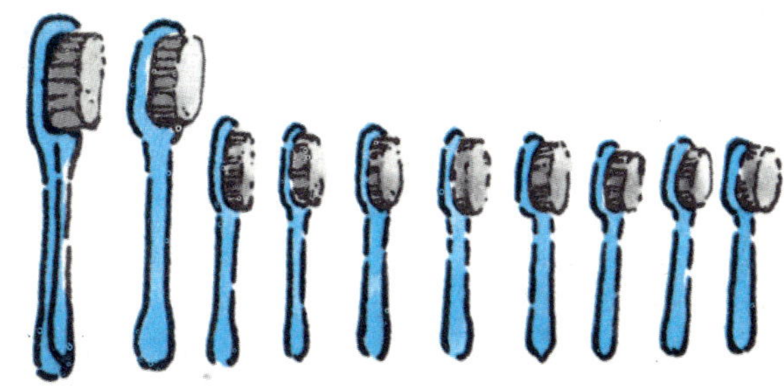

Die Zahnbürsten einer großen Familie
The toothbrushes of a large family
Die Familie hat acht Kinder.
There are eight children in the family.

Hier sind sieben Männer.
Here are seven men.

Hier sind drei Cowboys und vier Gangster.
There are three cowboys and four gangsters.

Wer gewinnt?
Who is winning?

Augusts

Heinrich Groß
Henry Gross
Moritz, Augusts Papagei
Maurice, August's parrot
Georg, der Zoowärter
George, the keeper at the zoo
Frau Jung
Mrs. Jung
Herr Groß
Mr. Gross
Fiffi, der Hund
Fiffi, the dog
Fräulein Braun
Miss Braun
Johannes
John

Freunde August's friends

Augusts Freunde
August's friends

August ist ein Landstreicher.
August is a tramp.
Er ist auch die Hauptperson dieses Buches.
He is also the hero of this book.
Hier sind einige seiner Freunde.
Here are some of his friends.

Moritz ist Augusts Papagei.
Maurice is August's parrot.
Er hat grüne Federn.
He has green feathers.
Er ist sehr stolz auf seine Federn.
He is very proud of his feathers.

Albert ist Augusts Kater.
Albert is August's cat.
Im Sommer bleibt Albert bei August.
In summer, Albert stays with August.
Aber im Winter ist es kalt.
But in winter it's cold.
Albert mag die Kälte nicht.
Albert doesn't like the cold.
Im Winter zieht Albert zu Frau Jung.
In winter, Albert goes to Mrs. Jung's house.

Frau Jung ist eine alte Freundin von August.
Mrs. Jung is an old friend of August's.
Sie überläßt August ihr Badezimmer und manchmal ihre Küche.
She lends August her bathroom and, sometimes, her kitchen.

Heinrich ist der Sohn von Herrn Groß.
Henry is Mr. Gross' son.
Heinrich ist sehr dünn.
Henry is very thin.
Er ist Eisverkäufer.
He is an ice-cream seller.
Manchmal schenkt er August ein Eis.
Sometimes he gives August an ice-cream.

Georg ist Wärter im Zoo.
George is the keeper at the zoo.
Georg gibt August oft eine Freikarte für den Zoo.
George often gives August a free ticket for the zoo.
August geht gern in den Zoo.
August loves going to the zoo.

Herr Groß ist Bäcker.
Mr. Gross is a baker.
Er ist sehr dick.
He is very fat.
Er ißt große Mengen von Brot und Kuchen.
He eats a lot of bread and cakes.
Manchmal schenkt er August etwas Kuchen.
Sometimes he gives August some cakes.

Fräulein Braun ist Lehrerin.
Miss Braun is a teacher.
Sie leiht August Bücher.
She lends August books.
Aber August kann nicht lesen.
But August can't read.
Fräulein Braun gibt August Leseunterricht.
Miss Braun gives August reading lessons.

Herr Rund ist Bauer.
Mr. Rund is a farmer.
Er hat einen Stall und viele Tiere.
He has a barn and a lot of animals.
Im Winter schläft August im Stall.
In Winter, August sleeps in the barn.

Professor Julius interessiert sich für die Sterne.
Professor Julius is interested in the stars.
Er sieht sie sich die ganze Nacht lang an.
He looks at them all night long.
Er spricht mit August über die Sterne.
He talks about the stars to August.

Sylvia ist Platzanweiserin im Kino.
Sylvia is an usherette at the movies.
Manchmal gibt sie August eine Freikarte.
Sometimes she gives August a free ticket.

Peter ist Astronaut.
Peter is an astronaut.
Er spricht mit August über den Mond.
He talks about the moon to August.
August möchte zum Mond fliegen.
August wants to go to the moon.

Frau Weiß ist Taxifahrerin.
Mrs. Weiss is a taxi-driver.
Manchmal nimmt sie August in ihrem Taxi mit.
Sometimes she gives August a ride in her taxi.

Jeremias ist ein Zigeuner.
Jeremy is a gypsy.
Er fängt viele Kaninchen.
He catches a lot of rabbits.
Oft gibt er August ein Kaninchen.
He often gives August a rabbit.

Marianne Rund ist die Tochter von Herrn Rund.
Marion Rund is Mr. Rund's daughter.
Sie kann nicht schwimmen.
She can't swim.
August gibt Marianne Schwimmunterricht.
August gives Marion swimming lessons.

Johannes schaut gerne bei Fußballspielen zu.
John loves watching soccer matches.
August begleitet ihn oft.
Often August goes with him.

Fiffi ist Augusts treuer Freund.
Fiffi is August's faithful friend.
Er bewacht August.
He guards August.
Aber wenn er Wache hält, schläft Fiffi oft ein.
But often, when he is on guard, Fiffi falls asleep.

August badet

August has a bath

Sie möchten . . . sein
They want to be . . .

Frau Jung möchte eine Ballerina sein.
Mrs. Jung wants to be a ballet dancer.

Herr Groß möchte vor allem dünn sein.
Mr. Gross wants first of all to be thin.
Und dann möchte er ein Cowboy sein.
Then he wants to be a cowboy.

Fiffi möchte ein Pudel sein.
Fiffi wants to be a poodle.
Er möchte Preise in Wettbewerben gewinnen.
He wants to win prizes in competitions.

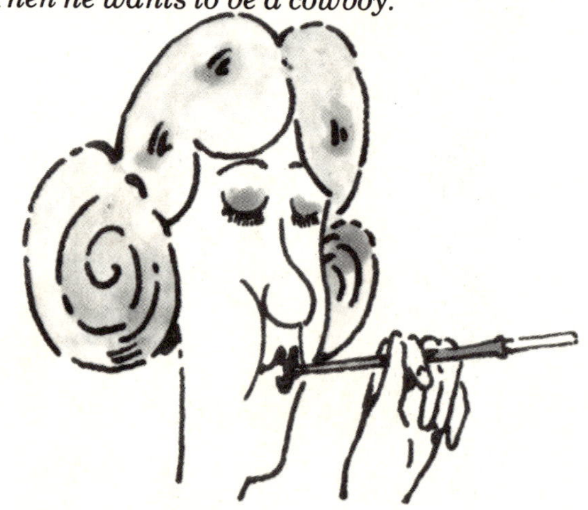

Fräulein Braun möchte Spionin sein.
Miss Braun wants to be a spy.
Sie möchte schön und gefährlich sein.
She wants to be beautiful and dangerous.

Jeremias möchte ein Pirat sein.
Jeremy wants to be a pirate.
Er möchte auf einem Schiff in weit entfernte Länder reisen.
He wants to go in a ship to far-off countries.

Georg möchte ein Maler sein.
George wants to be a painter.
Er möchte von allen Tieren im Zoo Porträts malen.
He wants to paint portraits of all the animals in the zoo.

Marianne Rund möchte Schlagersängerin sein.
Marion Rund wants to be a pop singer.

Professor Julius möchte Astronaut sein.
Professor Julius wants to be an astronaut.
Er möchte den Sternen näher sein.
He wants to be closer to the stars.

Herr Rund mag Geld.
Mr. Rund likes money.
Er möchte ein Millionär sein.
He wants to be a millionaire.

Peter hat von Mond und Sternen genug.
Peter has had enough of the moon and the stars.
Er möchte Unterwasserforscher sein.
He wants to be an under-water explorer.

Johannes möchte Berufsfußballspieler sein.
John wants to be a professional football player.
Oder ein Diskjockey.
Or a disc-jockey.

Frau Weiß hat genug davon, mit ihrem Taxi Leute herumzufahren.
Mrs. Weiss has had enough of driving people in her taxi.
Sie möchte reich sein.
She wants to be rich.
Sie möchte sich selbst Taxis nehmen können.
She wants to take taxis herself.

Im Zoo
At the zoo

Zwei Giraffen
Two giraffes
Die eine Giraffe heißt Gertrud.
One of the giraffes is called Gertrude.
Die andere heißt Karl.
The other one is called Charles.

Ein Löwe und eine Löwin
A lion and a lioness
Sie sind hungrig.
They are hungry.
Seehunde
Seals
Sie tauchen gern.
They love diving.
Ein Elefant
An elephant
Eine Schlange
A snake
Ein Krokodil
A crocodile
Der Elefantenrüssel
The elephant's trunk
Ein Flamingo
A flamingo
Herr Groß gibt den Pinguinen Kuchen.
Mr. Gross is giving the penguins some cakes.

Georg und Gertrud
George and Gertrude

Georg ist Wärter im Zoo.
George is a keeper at the zoo.
Er ist sehr besorgt.
He is very worried.

Gertrud, die Giraffe, weigert sich zu fressen.
Gertrude the giraffe refuses to eat.
Sie wird immer dünner.
She is getting thin.

Georg gibt Gertrud etwas Heu.
George gives Gertrude some hay.
Doch sie weigert sich, es zu fressen.
But she refuses to eat it.

Georg gibt Gertrud einige grüne Blätter.
George gives Gertrude some green leaves.
Sie weigert sich, sie zu fressen.
She refuses to eat them.
Sie wird dünner und dünner.
She is getting thinner and thinner.

Gertrud ist sehr, sehr dünn.
Gertrude is very, very thin.
Der Zoodirektor geht zu ihr.
The head of the zoo goes to see her.

„Hier, friß doch!" sagt der Zoodirektor zu Gertrud.
"Go on, eat!" says the head to Gertrude.
Doch sie weigert sich zu fressen.
But she refuses to eat.

Georg ist verzweifelt.
George is in despair.
Gertrud wird sterben.
Gertrude is going to die.

Doch Gertrud stirbt nicht.
But Gertrude doesn't die.
Nachts schlüpft sie durch das Gitter ihres Käfigs.
At night, she slips between the bars of her cage.

Gertrud ist frei!
Gertrude is free!

Sie ist sehr, sehr hungrig.
She is very, very hungry.

Sie frißt die Blätter von den Bäumen im Zoo.
She eats the leaves of the trees in the zoo.

Gertrud flieht.
Gertrude escapes.
Auf Wiedersehen, Zoo!
Good-bye zoo!

Gertrud ist sehr glücklich.
Gertrude is very happy.
Doch Georg und der Zoodirektor sind wütend.
But George and the head of the zoo are furious.

Im Kino   *At the cinema*

Die Cowboys tragen weiße Hüte.
The cowboys wear white hats.
Die Gangster tragen schwarze Hüte.
The gangsters wear black hats.

Ein roter Samtvorhang
A red velvet curtain

Eine Platzanweiserin
An usherette
Sie ist eine Freundin von Sylvia.
She is a friend of Sylvia's.

Sie verkauft Schokolade und Nüsse.
She is selling chocolate and nuts.
Was verkauft sie sonst noch?
What else is she selling?

Die Zuschauer
The audience

Frau Rund
Mrs. Rund
Sie mag Wildwestfilme gar nicht.
She hates westerns.
Sie fürchtet sich vor Gangstern.
She is afraid of the gangsters.

Herr Rund und Marianne
Mr. Rund and Marion
Sie mögen Wildwestfilme gern.
They love westerns.

August kommt herein.
August is coming in.
Er sieht sich gern Filme an.
He loves watching films.
AUSGANG
EXIT
Moritz, Albert und Fiffi
Maurice, Albert and Fiffi
Sie mögen Wildwestfilme gern.
They love westerns.
Aber sie dürfen nicht ins Kino hinein.
But they can't go into the cinema.
Eine Uhr
A clock
TOILETTEN
TOILETS
Sylvia nimmt die Karten.
Sylvia takes the tickets.
Eine Taschenlampe
A torch
Johannes
John
Er möchte Cowboy sein.
He wants to be a cowboy.

Wo wohnen sie?
Where do they live?

Das Baby steht in einem Laufgitter.
The baby lives in a cot.
Es mag sein Laufgitter gar nicht.
He hates his cot.

Die Marsmenschen leben auf dem Mars.
The Martians live on Mars.

Omi wohnt in einem Bungalow.
Granny lives in a bungalow.

Der Bär lebt in den Bergen.
The bear lives in the mountains.

Die Zwillinge wohnen in einem Wolkenkratzer.
The twins live in a skyscraper.
Sie wohnen im dreißigsten Stock.
They are on the thirtieth floor.

Georg wohnt in einem Baumhaus.
George lives in a tree-house.
Es ist nicht sehr stabil.
It's not very strong.

Die Mäuse leben in einem Loch.
The mice live in a hole.
Es ist sehr dunkel.
It's very dark.

Im Winter wohnt August unter einer Brücke.
In winter, August lives under a bridge.

Die Astronauten möchten auf dem Mond leben.
The astronauts want to live on the moon.

Im Sommer wohnt August unter einem Baum.
In summer, August lives under a tree.

Der Matrose lebt auf einem Schiff.
The sailor lives on a ship.
Manchmal ist er seekrank.
Sometimes he is sea-sick.

Der König wohnt in seinem Schloß.
The King lives in his castle.
Es ist ein bißchen kalt dort.
It's a bit cold there.

Der Schäfer wohnt in einer Hütte mit den Lämmern.
The shepherd lives in a hut, with the lambs.

Der Affe lebt im Urwald.
The monkey lives in the jungle.

Der Zigeuner wohnt in einem Zigeunerwagen.
The gypsy lives in a caravan.

Herr Groß in der Küche
Mr. Gross in the kitchen

Ein Stern
A star
Der Mond
The moon
Ein Kuckuck
A cuckoo
Es ist Mitternacht.
It's midnight.
Herr Groß ist im Schlafanzug.
Mr. Gross is in his pyjamas.
Er ist hungrig.
He is hungry.
Ein Glas Milch
A glass of milk
Eier
Eggs
Obst
Fruit
Käse
Cheese
Ein Kühlschrank
A refrigerator

August im Krankenhaus
August in hospital

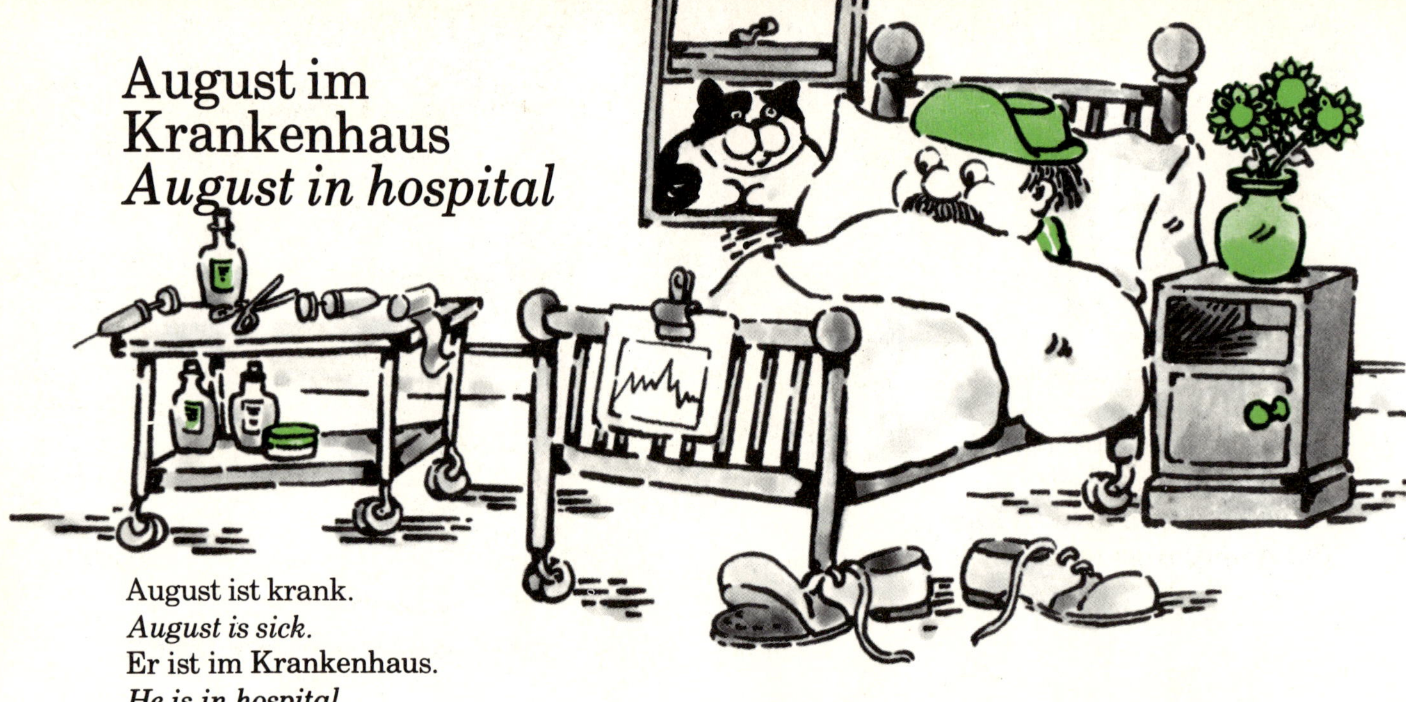

August ist krank.
August is sick.
Er ist im Krankenhaus.
He is in hospital.

Frau Jung besucht August.
Mrs. Jung visits August.
Sie bringt ihm ein paar Blumen.
She brings him some flowers.

Jeremias, der Zigeuner, kommt.
Jeremy the gypsy arrives.
Er bringt ein bißchen Kaninchensuppe.
He brings some rabbit soup.

Georg schenkt August ein Heft mit Eintrittskarten für den Zoo.
George gives August a book of tickets for the zoo.
August geht sehr gern in den Zoo.
August loves going to the zoo.

Herr Groß bringt eine große Schachtel.
Mr. Gross brings a huge box.
In der Schachtel sind sechs Kuchen.
In the box there are six cakes.

Fräulein Braun kommt.
Miss Braun arrives.
Sie bringt einige Bücher mit.
She brings some books.
Aber August kann nicht lesen.
But August can't read.

Sylvia schenkt August eine Filmzeitschrift.
Sylvia gives August a film magazine.
In der Zeitschrift sind Fotos von Filmschauspielern.
In the magazine there are photos of film stars.

Heinrich Groß bringt ein Eis mit.
Henry Gross brings an ice cream.
August muß das Eis sehr schnell essen!
August has to eat the ice-cream very quickly!

August ist von Geschenken umgeben.
August is surrounded by presents.
Er fühlt sich nicht mehr krank.
He doesn't feel sick any more.

Frau Weiß trifft mit ihrem Taxi ein.
Mrs. Weiss arrives in her taxi.
Sie bringt keine Geschenke.
She doesn't bring any presents.
Sie nimmt August mit!
She takes August away!

Vom Hubschrauber aus
From the helicopter

Der Hubschrauber
The helicopter
Der Pilot
The pilot
Er singt.
He is singing.
Er liebt das Fliegen.
He loves flying.
Der Passagier
The passenger
Ihm ist schlecht.
He is feeling air-sick.
Er möchte landen.
He wants to land.
Schornsteine
Chimneys
Schafe
Sheep
Eine Fabrik
A factory
Eine Brücke
A bridge
Ein Fluß
A river
Ein Lastwagen
A truck
Ein Pferd
A horse
Ein Zug
A train

Wenn ich Millionär wäre. . .

If I were a millionaire . . .

. . .würde ich um die Welt reisen.
I would go round the world.

. . .würde ich mir eine Insel kaufen.
I would buy an island.

. . .würde ich jeden Tag zwölf Portionen Eis essen.
I would eat twelve ice-creams every day.

. . .würde ich mir einen Zug kaufen und ihn selbst fahren.
I would buy a train and drive it.

. . .würde ich mit meinen Freunden in einem Wald leben.
I would live in a forest with my friends.

. . .würde ich ein Haus auf dem Meeresgrund haben.
I would have a house under the sea.

. . .würde ich mir tausend Luftballons kaufen und davonfliegen.
I would buy a thousand balloons and I would fly.

. . .würde ich auf den Mond fliegen.
I would go to the moon.

. . .würde ich in einem Zigeunerwagen leben. . .
I would live in a gypsy caravan . . .

. . .würde ich jeden Tag in den Zirkus gehen.
I would go to the circus every day.

. . .oder vielleicht in einem modernen Wohnwagen.
. . . or perhaps in a modern caravan.

Schwimmen *Swimming*

Die Sonne
The sun
Ein Hubschrauber
A helicopter
Ein Baum
A tree
Eine Kuh
A cow
Sie frißt gerade Augusts Unterhosen.
She is eating August's pants.
Augusts Hosen
August's trousers
Augusts Hund Fiffi
August's dog Fiffi
Er bewacht Augusts Kleidung.
He is guarding August's clothes.
Augusts Hut
August's hat
Augusts Hemd
August's shirt
Eine Ente
A duck
Eine Libelle
A dragon-fly
Sie beobachtet August.
It is watching August.
Ein Frosch
A frog
Er beobachtet die Libelle.
It is watching the dragon-fly.

August sieht fern
August looks at television

August hat keinen Fernseher.
August hasn't got television.
Aber er sieht gern fern.
But he loves watching television.

August geht in die Stadt.
August goes into town.
Er findet einen Fernseher.
He finds a television set.

Er sieht sich einen Wildwestfilm an.
He watches a western.

Er macht die Sänger nach.
He imitates the singers.

Dann sieht er ein Pop-Programm.
Then he watches a pop programme.

Er macht auch die Schauspieler nach. . .
He also imitates the comedians . . .

und er macht den Dirigenten nach. . .
and he imitates the conductors . . .

und er macht die Sportler nach. . .
and he imitates the sportsmen . . .

und er macht die Köche nach. . .
and he imitates the cooks . . .

und er macht die Tänzer nach. . .
and he imitates the dancers.

August sieht gern fern.
August loves watching television.
Und die Leute sehen gern August zu.
And people love watching August!

Eine Landkarte
A map

Bilder
Paintings
Welches Bild ist das beste?
Which painting is the best?

Blumen
Flowers

Ein Engländer ißt gerade Fisch und Pommes Frites.
An Englishman eating fish and chips.

Steine
Stones

Mariannes grüner Stein
Marion's green stone
Sie sagt, es sei
ein wertvoller Stein.
She says it is
a precious stone.

Mariannes Maus mag Fernsehen nicht.
Marion's mouse doesn't like television.

Bücher
Books
Wie viele Bücher kannst du hier im Klassenraum sehen?
How many books can you see in the classroom?

Ein Schreibheft
An exercise book

Ein Radiergummi
A rubber

Ein Kugelschreiber
A biro

Ein Lineal
A ruler

Ein Bleistift
A pencil

Kaugummi
Chewing-gum

Marianne Rund in der Schule
Marion Rund at school

Fräulein Braun
Miss Braun
Sie ist Lehrerin.
She is a teacher.

Marianne Rund mag den Englischunterricht.
Marion Rund likes English lessons.
Sie sieht gern fern.
She likes watching television.

Anne fürchtet sich vor Mäusen.
Anne is afraid of mice.
Sie wird gleich schreien.
She is going to scream.

Insekten
Insects

Johannes sieht gern fern – aber nur, wenn Fußball gezeigt wird.
John likes television – but only when there is football on.
Er liest eine Fußballzeitschrift.
He is reading a football magazine.

Wer ist hier gegangen?
Who has walked this way?

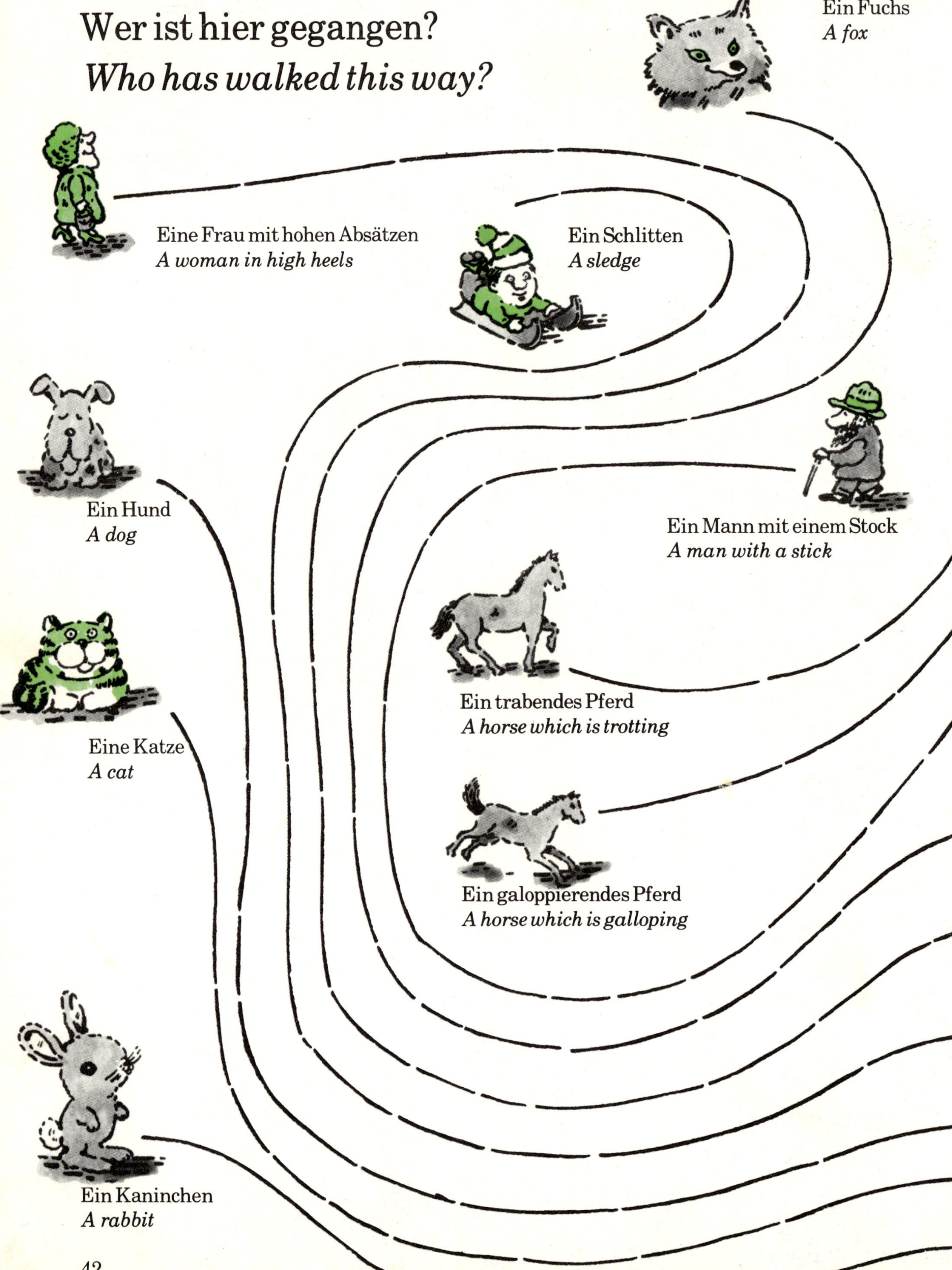

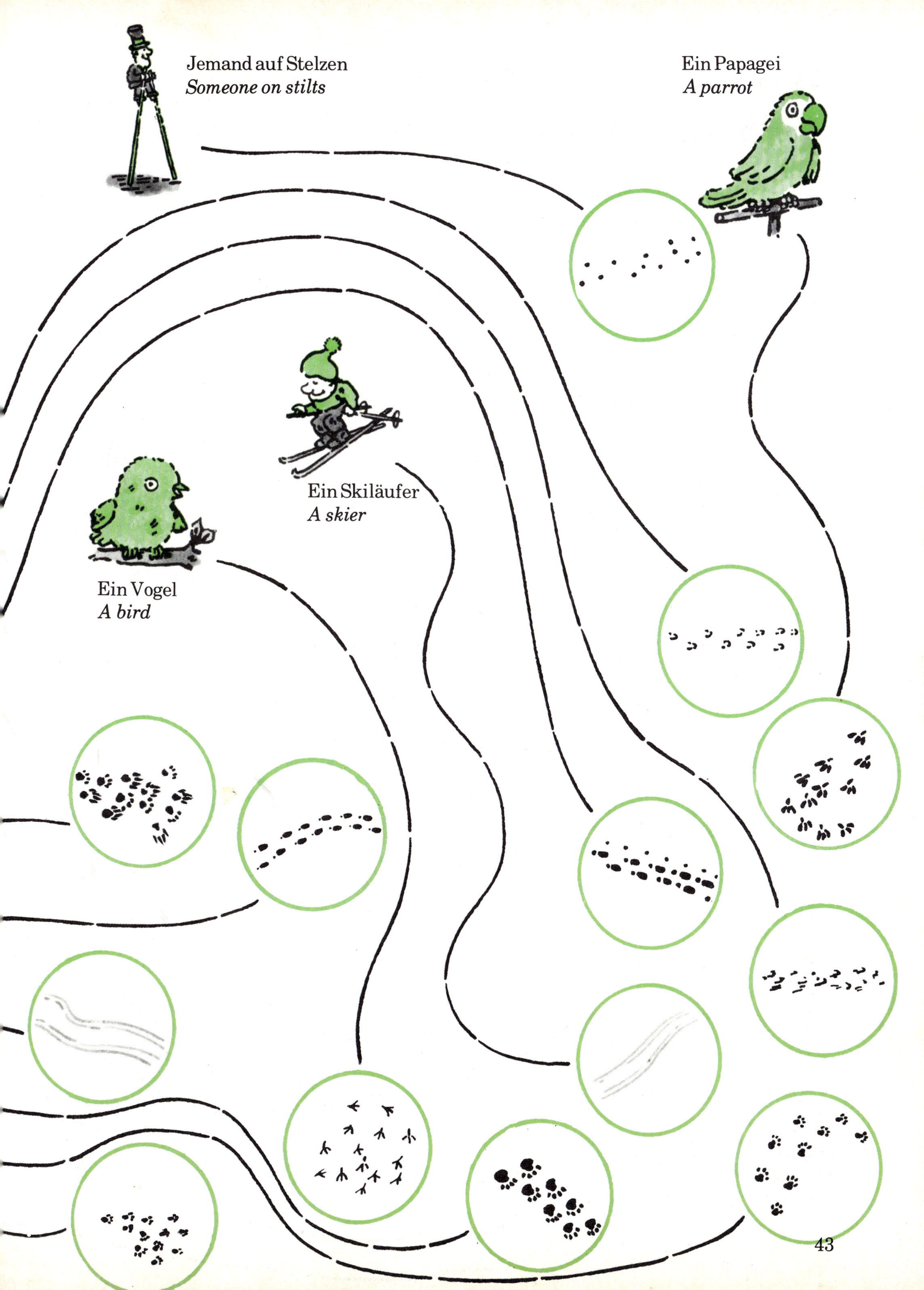
Jemand auf Stelzen
Someone on stilts
Ein Papagei
A parrot
Ein Skiläufer
A skier
Ein Vogel
A bird

Jeremias geht zu Bett
Jeremy goes to bed

Jeremias ist in seinem Zigeunerwagen.
Jeremy is in his caravan.
Draußen ist es kalt.
Outside it is cold.
Jeremias ist warm.
Jeremy is warm.

Jeremias' Mantel ist zerrissen.
Jeremy's coat is torn.
Er flickt ihn.
He is mending it.

Ein Wecker
An alarm clock
Er geht nicht, aber Jeremias mag ihn trotzdem.
It doesn't work, but Jeremy likes it.

Jeremias' Schlafanzug
Jeremy's pyjamas

Jeremias' Bett
Jeremy's bed

Jeremias' Hund
Jeremy's dog
Er heißt Böse.
He's called Wicked.
Er schaut nach der Brotschnitte.
He is looking at the sandwich.

Ein Butterbrot mit
Kaninchenfleisch.
A rabbit sandwich.

Ein glückbringendes Hufeisen
A lucky horseshoe
Ein Pullover
A sweater
Eine Kerze
A candle
Ein Fernseher
A television set
Er funktioniert nicht, aber Jeremias
mag ihn trotzdem.
It doesn't work, but Jeremy likes it.
Etwas Käse
Some cheese
Eine Maus
A mouse
Eine Weste
A waistcoat
Jeremias hat diese Weste im
Abfalleimer eines großen Hotels gefunden.
Jeremy found this waistcoat in the dustbin of a big hotel.

Frau Jungs Kuchen

Mrs. Jung's cake

Frau Jung ist in ihrer Küche.
Mrs. Jung is in her kitchen.
Sie macht einen Kuchen aus Eiern, Mehl, Butter und Milch.
She is making a cake with eggs, flour, butter and milk.

Frau Jung schiebt den Kuchen in den Ofen.
Mrs. Jung puts the cake in the oven.
Albert sieht zu.
Albert looks at it.

Sobald der Kuchen fertig ist, belegt ihn Frau Jung mit ein paar Kirschen.
When the cake is cooked, Mrs. Jung puts some cherries on it.

Frau Jung geht aus der Küche.
Mrs. Jung goes out of the kitchen.
Moritz, der Papagei kommt herein.
Maurice the parrot comes in.
Er frißt die Kirschen und fliegt davon.
He eats the cherries and flies away.

Frau Jung kommt in die Küche zurück.
Mrs. Jung comes back into the kitchen.
Wie schrecklich!
How terrible!
Wer hat die Kirschen gegessen?
Who has eaten the cherries?
Das muß Albert gewesen sein.
It must be Albert.

Frau Jung überzieht den Kuchen mit Schokolade.
Mrs. Jung covers the cake with chocolate.
Sie legt eine Kirsche in die Mitte.
She puts one cherry in the middle.
Sie schickt Albert aus der Küche.
She takes Albert out of the kitchen.

Moritz frißt die Kirsche.
Maurice eats the cherry.

Frau Jung kommt zurück.
Mrs. Jung comes back.
Auf dem Kuchen sieht sie eine Spur: Moritz' Krallen.
On the cake she sees a mark: Maurice's claw.

Frau Jung nimmt einen Kochtopf.
Mrs. Jung takes a saucepan.
Sie sucht Moritz...
She is going to look for Maurice...

Ein Schmetterling
A butterfly
Frül
In the
Ein Baum
A tree
Einige Zwerge
Some gnomes
Sind sie lebendig?
Are they alive?
Laubblätter
Leaves
Eine Schaukel
A swing
Ein Rasen
A lawn
Ein Goldfisch
A goldfish
Er schläft.
It is asleep.
Ein Maulwur
A mol
Er schläft
It is asleep
Rosen
Roses
Ein Maulwurfshaufe
A mole-hil
Tau
Dew

[m]orgens im Garten
[in the g]arden early in the morning

Die Sonne geht auf.
The sun is rising.

Eine Hecke
A hedge

Eine Feldmaus
A field-mouse
Wie viele Junge sind es?
How many babies are there?

Ein Vogel
A bird
Er nimmt sein Morgenbad.
He is having his morning bath.

Narzissen
Daffodils

Tulpen
Tulips

Eine Raupe
A caterpillar
Wie viele Raupen kannst du sehen?
How many caterpillars can you see?

Ein Eichhörnchen
A squirrel
Es geht, um Nüsse zu suchen.
He is going to find some nuts.

Geschenke
Presents

Ein Meerschweinchen
A guinea pig

Ein Astronautenanzug
An astronaut costume

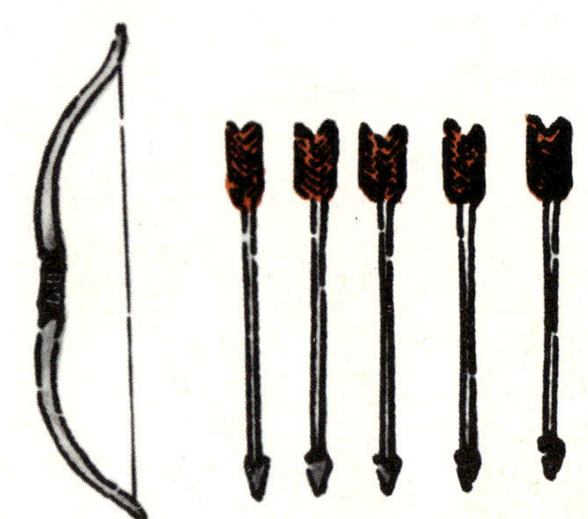

Ein Bogen und Pfeile
A bow and arrows

Ein Farbtopf
A pot of paint

Bücher
Books

Eine Kamera
A camera
Wen kannst du auf dem Foto sehen?
Who can you see in the photo?

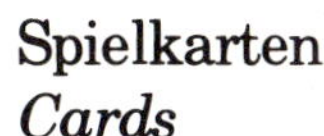

Spielkarten
Cards

Blumensamen
Flower seeds

Ein Sparschwein – und etwas Geld
A money box – and some money.

Masken
Masks

Eine Marionette
A puppet

Ein Rückenkratzer
A back-scratcher

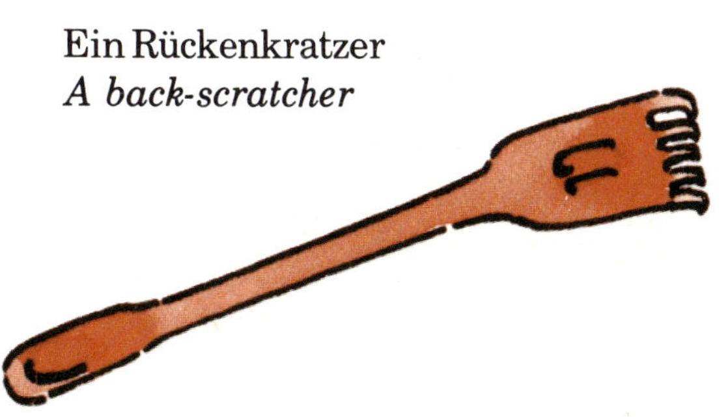

Ein junger Hund
A puppy
Gib ihm einen Namen.
Give him a name.

Ein Kanu
A canoe

Ein Drachen
A kite

Ein Fahrrad
A bicycle

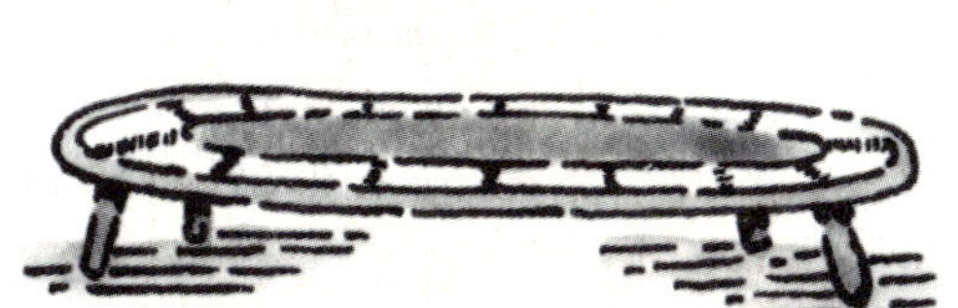

Ein Trampolin
A trampoline

Kakao
Cocoa
Zucker
Sugar
Flüssige Schokolade
Liquid chocolate
Nüsse
Nuts
Ein Kittel
An overall
Karamelbonbons
Caramels
Orangen-Pralinen
Orange creams
Kaffee-Pralinen
Coffee creams
Schuljungen und Schulmädchen
Schoolboys and schoolgirls
Wen kannst du erkennen?
Whom do you recognize?

In der Schokoladenfabrik
In the chocolate factory

August und Johannes gehen zu einem Fußballspiel
August and John go to a football match

August und Johannes mögen Fußball.
August and John love football.
Sie gehen zusammen zu einem Spiel.
They are going to a match together.

Die *Löwen* spielen gegen die *Schwarzen Hunde.*
The Lions *are playing the* Black Dogs.
Beide Vereine sind sehr stark.
Both teams are very strong.

Im Stadion ist eine riesige Menschenmenge.
In the stadium there is an enormous crowd.

August und Johannes schreien, um die *Schwarzen Hunde* anzufeuern.
August and John shout to encourage the Black Dogs.

Das Spiel beginnt.
The match begins.
Die *Schwarzen Hunde* laufen sehr schnell.
The Black Dogs *run very fast.*

Der Kapitän der *Schwarzen Hunde* schießt ein Tor.
The captain of the Black Dogs *is going to score a goal.*

Es ist ein Tor!
It's a goal!
Aber der Ball fliegt weiter!
But the ball doesn't stop!
Er landet auf Augusts Kopf!
It lands on August's head!

August ist betäubt.
August is dazed.

August und Johannes gehen zum Ausgang.
August and John go to the exit.
Der Direktor des Stadions kommt.
The manager of the stadium arrives.

Er überreicht August und Johannes Freikarten
für ein wichtiges Spiel in der nächsten Woche.
He gives August and John free tickets for the big match next week.
August und Johannes freuen sich sehr!
August and John are very pleased!

August am Strand

August at the seaside

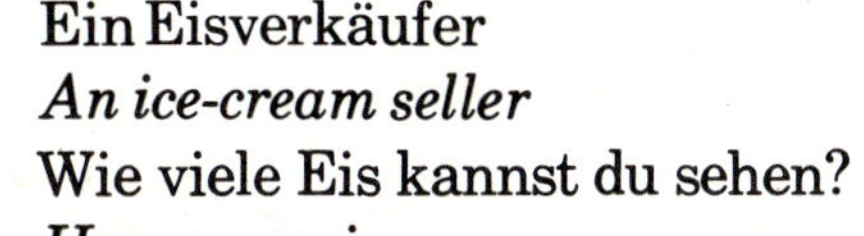

Ein Eisverkäufer
An ice-cream seller
Wie viele Eis kannst du sehen?
How many ice-creams can you see?

Marianne Rund lernt schwimmen.
Marion Rund is learning to swim.

Coca-Cola Flaschen
Bottles of Coca-cola

Ein Badeanzug
A bathing suit

Ein Papierhut
A paper hat

Diese Frau sieht dem Hund zu.
This woman is looking at the dog

Muscheln
Shells

Ein Plastikdrachen
A plastic dragon

Ein Gummiknochen
A rubber bone

Ein Eimer
A bucket

Die Kinder bauen Sandburgen.
The children are making sand-castles.

In den Ferien
On holiday

Am Meer
At the seaside
Suche einen Spaten, einen Eimer und fünf Muscheln.
Find a spade, a bucket and five shells.

Auf einem Kanal
On a canal
Möchtest du auf einem Flußschiff leben?
Would you like to live on a barge?

Im Winter in den Bergen
In the mountains in winter
Wer läuft Ski?
Who is ski-ing?
Weißt du, wie man skiläuft?
Do you know how to ski?

Auf dem Lande
In the country
Hast du Picknicks gern?
Do you like picnics?
Wie ist das Wetter?
What is the weather like?

Im Sommer in den Bergen
In the mountains in summer
Die Sonne scheint, aber es liegt immer noch etwas Schnee.
The sun is shining but there is still some snow.

Auf einer verlassenen Insel
On a desert island
Sind Häuser auf der Insel?
Are there any houses on the island?

Im Urwald
In the jungle
Es regnet.
It's raining.
Die Papageien stellen sich unter die Bäume.
The parrots go under the trees.

Auf einem See
On a lake
Ist es Winter oder Sommer?
Is it winter or summer?

Beim Friseur

Fräulein Jette wäscht dieser Frau die Haare.
Miss Jane is washing this woman's hair.
Die Frau sagt, daß das Wasser zu heiß ist.
The woman says that the water is too hot.

Sylvia hat sehr lockiges Haar.
Sylvia has very curly hair.
Sie hätte lieber glattes Haar.
She prefers straight hair.

Fräulein Braun mag ihr Haar nicht.
Miss Braun doesn't like her hair.
Sie möchte es anders haben.
She wants to change it.
Sie sucht sich eine Perücke aus.
She is choosing a wig.

Nagellack
Nail polish

Ein Kamm
A comb

Ein Haarnetz
A hair-net

At the hairdresser's

Frau Jung ist unter der Trockenhaube.
Mrs. Jung is under the dryer.
Sie liest Zeitschriften.
She is reading magazines.

Wie furchtbar!
How terrible!
Das Haar von Frau Weiß ist grün geworden.
Mrs. Weiss' hair has gone green!

Fräulein Anne manikürt diese Frau.
Miss Anne is giving this woman a manicure.

Eine Haarbürste
A hairbrush

Haarfestiger
Lacquer

Lockenwickler
Rollers

Fräulein Braun kauft einen Hund.

Miss Braun buys a dog.

Fräulein Braun möchte einen Hund kaufen.
Miss Braun wants to buy a dog.

Sie geht in eine Tierhandlung.
She goes to a pet-shop.

Das Geschäft ist voller Tiere.
The shop is full of animals.

Da gibt es Hamster, Meerschweinchen, weiße Mäuse, Katzen, Kanarienvögel, Kaninchen und Hunde.
There are hamsters, guinea pigs, white mice, cats, canaries, rabbits, and dogs.

Fräulein Braun sieht sich die Hunde an.
Miss Braun looks at the dogs.

Sie sucht sich einen kleinen schwarzen Hund aus.
She chooses a small black dog.

Der Hund beißt Fräulein Braun.
The dog bites Miss Braun.

Fräulein Braun möchte nun keinen Hund haben.
Miss Braun doesn't want a dog any longer.

Statt eines Hundes sucht sie sich vier Goldfischgläser aus.
Instead of a dog, she chooses four bowls of goldfish.

Fräulein Braun ist glücklich.
Miss Braun is happy.

Goldfische beißen nicht.
Goldfish don't bite.

Das Hockeyspiel

Die Mädchen haben vier Tore geschossen.
The girls have scored four goals.
Die Jungen haben nur ein Tor geschossen.
The boys have scored only one goal.

Die Zuschauer
The spectators

Alle schreien „Hurra!"
They are all shouting, "Hooray!"
Die Jungen schreien nicht so laut wie die Mädchen.
The boys are shouting less loudly than the girls.

Zitronen für die Halbzeit
Lemons for half-time

Der Schiedsrichter
The referee
Er ist viel gelaufen.
He has been running a lot.

Kurze Hosen
Shorts

Die Spielführerin der Mädchenmannschaft
The captain of the girls' team
Sie freut sich sehr.
She is very pleased.

The hockey match

Der Ball ist weit weg gerollt.
The ball has gone a long way away.
Fiffi sucht den Ball.
Fiffi want to find the ball.

Die Sportlehrerin der Mädchenschule freut sich sehr.
The sports mistress of the girls' school is very pleased.

Sie ist sehr stolz auf ihre Mannschaft.
She is very proud of her team.

Ist das ein Mädchen oder ein Junge?
Is this a girl or a boy?
Woran siehst du das?
How do you know?

Ein Hockeyschläger
A hockey stick

Ein Sporthemd
A sports shirt

Der Kapitän der Jungenmannschaft
The captain of the boys' team
Er ist wütend.
He is furious.
Er tut so, als ob er sich erfreut.
He is pretending to be pleased.

Ich möchte . . . werden
I'm going to be . . .

Ein Reporter
A reporter

Eine Köchin
A cook

Ein Mannequin
A model

Eine Hausfrau
A housewife

Ein Schlagersänger
A pop singer

Ein Arzt
A doctor

Eine Fernsehreporterin
A television interviewer

Eine Stewardeß
An air hostess

Ein Berufsfußballspieler
A professional football player

Ein Entdecker
An explorer

Ein Zoowärter
A keeper at the zoo

Ein Jockei
A jockey

Ein Briefträger
A postman

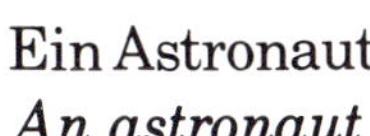

Ein Astronaut
An astronaut

Ein Schauspieler
An actor

Ein Pilot
A pilot

Ein Mechaniker
A mechanic

Ein Maurer
A builder

Der Dirigent
The conductor
In der Hand hat er einen weißen Taktstock.
In his hand he has a white baton.
Er sieht die Geiger wütend an.
He is looking at the violinists with fury.
Sie spielen schlecht.
They are playing badly.

Der erste Geiger
The first violinist
Er kann den Dirigenten nicht leiden.
He does not like the conductor.

Der Pianist
The pianist

Der Sänger
The male singer
Er hat eine ziemlich schwache Stimme.
He has a rather weak voice.
Er fürchtet sich vor der Sängerin.
He is afraid of the lady singer.

Ein Konzert *A concert*

Die Pauken
Drums

Ein Horn
A French horn

Ein Cello
A double-bass
Der Cellist ist sehr klein.
The double-bass player is very small.
Er kann den Dirigenten nicht sehr gut sehen.
He can't see the conductor very well.

Ohrringe
Earrings

Eine Diamantenhalskette
A diamond necklace
Es sind keine echten Diamenten.
They are not real diamonds.

Ein rotes Kleid
A red dress

Die Sängerin
The lady singer
Sie hat eine sehr kräftige Stimme
She has a very powerful voice.

Goldschuhe
Gold shoes

August geht zur Autoausstellung
August goes to the Motor Show

August kann nicht Auto fahren.
August can't drive a car.

Aber er interessiert sich für Autos.
But he is interested in cars.

Er entschließt sich, zu einer Autoausstellung zu gehen.
He decides to go to the Motor Show.

Aber August hat kein Geld.
But August has no money.
Er kann den Eintrittspreis nicht bezahlen.
He can't pay the entrance fee.

Aber plötzlich kommt ein Mann daher.
But suddenly a man comes along.

Er schüttelt Augusts Hand.
He shakes August's hand.

August weiß nicht weshalb.
August doesn't know why.

Der Mann sagt: „Sie sind der millionste Besucher der Autoausstellung!"
The man says: "You are the millionth visitor to the Motor Show!"

„Sie haben einen Preis gewonnen!"
"You have won a prize!"

Der Mann zeigt August seinen Preis.
The man shows August his prize.

Es ist ein riesengroßes Auto.
It is a huge car.

August sieht Frau Weiß.
August sees Mrs. Weiss.

Beide steigen in das Auto.
They both get into the car.

August verläßt die Autoausstellung.
August leaves the Motor Show.

Aber er hat den Eintrittspreis immer noch nicht bezahlt!
But he still hasn't paid the entrance fee!

Auf dem Spielplatz
In the playground

Dieser Junge spielt nicht gern.
This boy doesn't like playing.
Er liest lieber.
He prefers reading.
Er liest eine Sportzeitschrift.
He's reading a sports magazine.

Drei Mädchen spielen „Himmel und Hölle".
Three girls are playing hopscotch.

Dieses Mädchen hat ein neues Springtau bekommen.
This girl has got a new skipping-rope.
Es kann dreihundertmal hintereinander hüpfen, ohne aufzuhöre
She can do three hundred skips without stopping.

Dieses Mädchen macht Schularbeiten.
This girl is doing her homework.

Marianne Rund schnallt ihre Rollschuhe an.
Marion Rund is putting on her roller skates.

Diese Mädchen spielen Verstecken.
These girls are playing hide and seek.
Suche das Mädchen, das sich versteckt hat.
Find the girl who is hiding.

Dieser Junge raucht eine Zigarette.
This boy is smoking a cigarette.
Welche Farbe hat sein Gesicht?
What colour is his face?

Johannes spielt mit seinen Freunden Fußball.
John is playing football with his friends.

Diese beiden Jungen sind hungrig.
These two boys are hungry.
Was essen sie?
What are they eating?

Eltern und Kinder
Parents and children

Heinrich Groß ist dünn.
Henry Gross is thin.
Sein Vater, Herr Groß, ist dick.
His father, Mr. Gross, is fat.
Seine Mutter, Frau Groß, ist weder dick noch dünn.
His mother, Mrs. Gross, is neither fat nor thin.

Hier sind vier Würmer: Großvater, Vater, Sohn und Enkel.
Here are four worms: grandfather, father, son and grandson.
Welcher ist der Vater?
Which is the father?

Dieser Riese ist sehr groß.
This giant is very tall.
Seine Tochter ist sehr klein.
His daughter is very short.
Sie ist ein Baby.
She is a baby.

Dieses Kängeruh hat sein Kind im Beutel.
This kangaroo has its child in its pouch.

Dieses Lamm hat keine Mutter.
This lamb has no mother.
Der Schäfer gibt ihm etwas Milch.
The shepherd gives it some milk.

Die Mutter dieses jungen Hundes ist ein Pudel.
This puppy's mother is a poodle.
Sein Vater ist ein Boxer.
His father is a boxer.
Der junge Hund ist weder ein Pudel noch ein Boxer.
The puppy is neither a poodle nor a boxer.

Hier sind ein Mann, seine Frau, sein Sohn, seine Tochter und sein Hund.
Here are a man, his wife, his son, his daughter and his dog.
Sie sind sich alle ähnlich.
They look like one another.

Peter fliegt zum Mond
Peter goes to the moon

Ein Foto von Peters Freundin
A photo of Peter's girl friend

Ein Foto von Peters Vater und Mutter
A photo of Peter's father and mother

Ein Foto vom Entdecker des Raumschiffes
A photo of the inventor of the spacecraft

Peters Tee
Peter's tea

Peters Mittagessen
Peter's lunch

Peters Frühstück
Peter's breakfast

Der Himmel ist dunkelblau.
The sky is dark blue.

Sterne
Stars

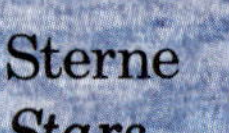

Professor Julius sieht das Raumschiff durch sein Fernglas.
Professor Julius is looking at the spacecraft through his telescope.
Er würde sehr gern zum Mond fliegen.
He would love to go to the moon.

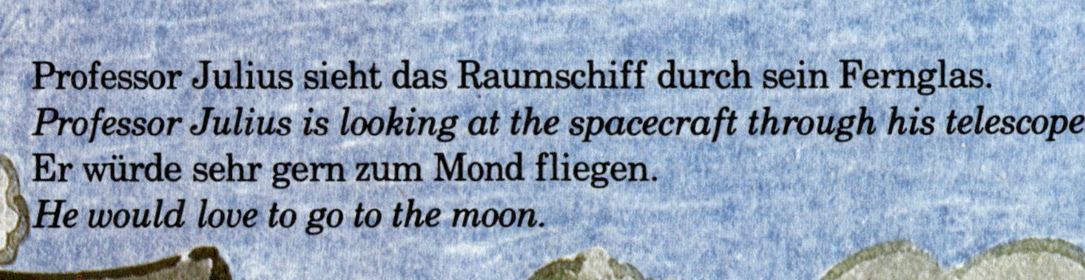

Ein bißchen Erde
A bit of earth
Peter wird es auf dem Mond lassen.
Peter is going to put it on the moon.
Der Mond
The moon
Er ist noch sehr weit entfernt.
It is still a long way away.
Die Betriebsanleitung
The instruction book
Der Geschwindigkeitsmesser
The speedometer
Peter fliegt immer schneller.
Peter is going faster and faster.
Er fliegt gern schnell.
He loves going fast.
Das Raumschiff
The spacecraft

Frau Jung sucht sich einen Hut aus

Mrs. Jung chooses a hat

Frau Jung möchte sich einen neuen Hut kaufen.
Mrs. Jung wants to buy herself a new hat.
Die Auswahl ist groß.
There is a big choice.

Sie probiert einen großen Hut auf.
She tries on a big hat.

Dann setzt sie sich einen kleinen Hut auf.
Next she puts on a small hat.

Frau Jung mag schwarz sehr gern.
Mrs. Jung loves black.
Sie setzt sich einen schwarzen Hut mit Schleier auf.
She puts on a black hat with a veil.

Die Verkäuferin sucht einen Blumenhut aus.
The salesgirl chooses a hat covered with flowers.
Frau Jung mag ihn nicht.
Mrs. Jung doesn't like it.

Frau Jung probiert einen Plastikhut auf.
Mrs. Jung tries on a plastic hat.
Er steht ihr nicht.
It doesn't suit her.

Frau Jung kann keinen Hut finden.
Mrs. Jung can't find a hat.

Plötzlich bemerkt Frau Jung einen Hut mit Federn.
Suddenly, Mrs. Jung notices a hat with feathers.
Er ist genau richtig!
It is perfect!

Aber es ist der Hut einer anderen Frau.
But it's another woman's hat.

Frau Jung gibt der Frau etwas Geld.
Mrs. Jung gives the woman some money.
Beide freuen sich sehr.
Both of them are very pleased.

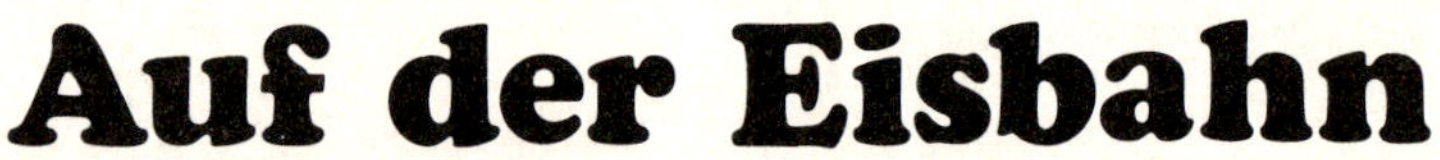

Auf der Eisbahn

August versucht sich Schlittschuhe anzuziehen.
August is trying to put on some skates.
Er will nicht Schlittschuh laufen.
He doesn't want to skate.
Er fürchtet sich davor, hinzufallen.
He is afraid of falling down.

Albert sieht den Schlittschuhläufern gern zu.
Albert likes watching the skaters.

Herr Groß ist zu dick zum Schlittschuhlaufen.
Mr. Gross is too fat to skate.
Er läuft Schlittschuh, weil er dünner werden will.
He skates because he wants to get thin.

Fräulein Braun läuft nicht gut Schlittschuh.
Miss Braun doesn't skate very well.
Sie versucht, es aus einem Buch zu lernen.
She is trying to learn from a book.

Sylvia läuft sehr schlecht Schlittschuh.
Sylvia skates very badly.
Aber sie hat viele Freunde.
But she has a lot of friends.
Die helfen ihr.
They help her.

At the ice-rink

Herr Rund sieht Marianne zu.
Mr. Rund is watching Marion.
Er ist sehr stolz auf sie.
He is very proud of her.

Ein kurzer Rock
A short skirt

Diese Dame ist eine Russin.
This lady is Russian.
Sie lernte Schlittschuhlaufen, als sie zwei Jahre alt war.
She learned to skate when she was two years old.

Marianne Rund läuft sehr gut Schlittschuh.
Marion Rund skates very well.
Sie kann tanzen.
She can dance.
Es ist schwierig, Marianne zu erkennen.
It is difficult to watch Marion.

Der Schlittschuhlehrer
The skating teacher
Er ist sehr eingebildet.
He is very conceited.

Schlittschuhe
Skates

Skelette
Skeletons

Suche das Bild, das zu jedem Skelett gehört.
Find the drawing which goes with each skeleton.

Ein Dinosaurier
A dinosaur
Es gibt keine Dinosaurier mehr.
There are no more dinosaurs.

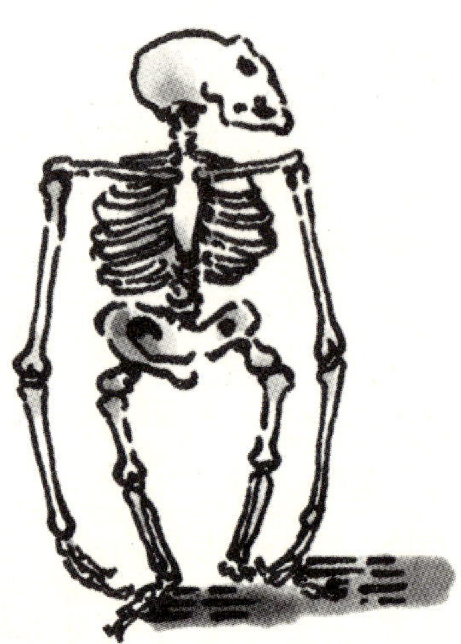

Ein Gorilla
A gorilla
Sein Skelett sieht aus wie das nächste Skelett.
Its skeleton looks like the next skeleton.

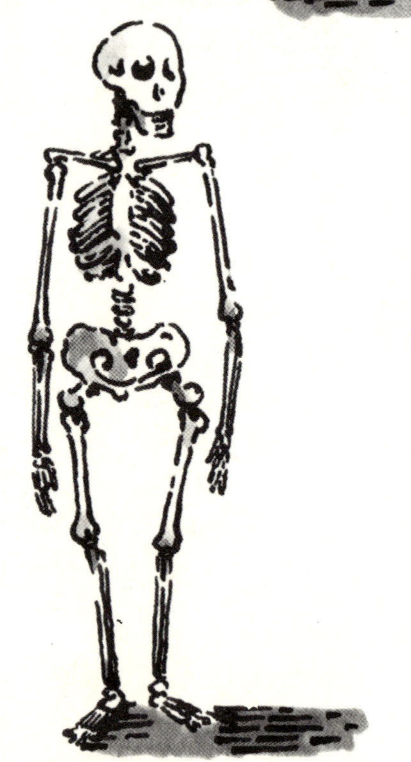

Ein Mensch
A man
Wie viele Knochen kannst du sehen?
How many bones can you see?

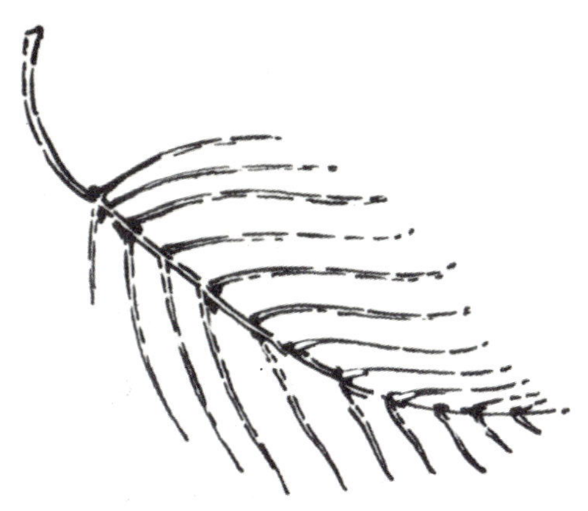

Ein Blatt
A leaf
Das sind die Adern eines Blattes.
Here are the veins of a leaf.

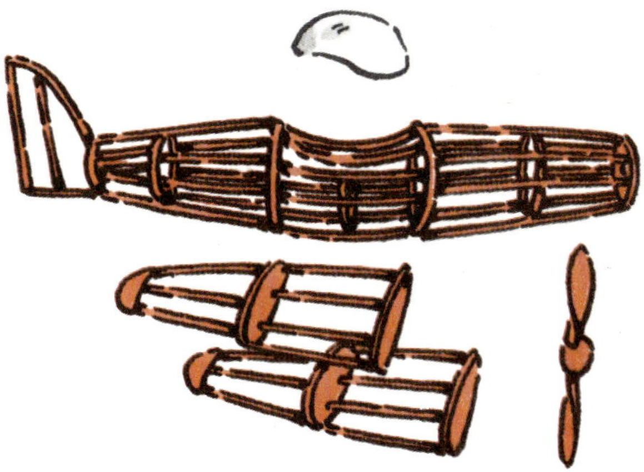

Ein Flugzeug
An aeroplane
Dies ist ein Modell.
This is a model.

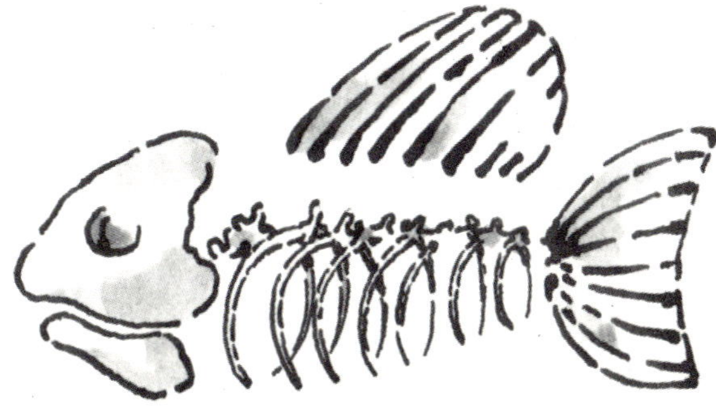

Ein Fisch
A fish
Ich glaube, es ist ein Hering.
I think it is a herring.

Auf der Rolltreppe

Jeremias, der Zigeuner
Jeremy, the gypsy
Was hat er unter dem Arm?
What has he got under his arm?

August sieht sich die Plakate an.
August is looking at the advertisements.
Er sieht ein Bild von einem großen Bett.
He sees a picture of a big bed.
August hat kein Bett.
August has no bed.

Albert mag die Rolltreppe nicht.
Albert does not like the escalator.

Moritz braucht keine Treppen.
Maurice doesn't need a staircase.
Er fliegt über alles hinweg.
He flies above everybody.

Ein Pelzmantel
A fur coat

Ein Einkaufskorb
A shopping basket

Ein Regenschirm
An umbrella

Diese Frau ist sehr überrascht, einen Papagei zu sehen.
This woman is very surprised to see a parrot.

On the escalator

Johannes versucht, die Aufwärtstreppe hinunterzugehen.
John is trying to go down the up staircase.

Eine Großmutter
A grandmother
Sie mag die Rolltreppe nicht.
She hates the escalator.
Sie geht ihr zu schnell.
It goes too fast.

Handschuhe
Gloves

Ein Großvater
A grandfather
Er versucht, seiner Frau zu helfen.
He is trying to help his wife.

Eine Handtasche
A handbag

Ein Filzhut
A bowler hat

Ein großer Koffer
A large suitcase

Ein Mantel
An overcoat

Jemand versucht, dem Großvater zu helfen.
Somebody is trying to help the grandfather.

Frau Jung und August backen Brot

Mrs. Jung and August make bread

Frau Jung und August backen Brot.
Mrs. Jung and August are making bread.
Sie mischen Mehl, Wasser und Salz.
They mix together flour, water and salt.

August versucht, das Rezept zu lesen.
August tries to read the recipe.

Frau Jung tut zwei Löffel Hefe dazu.
Mrs. Jung puts in two spoonfuls of yeast.

Sie stellen das Brot auf die Heizung.
They put the bread on the radiator.

Das Brot wird um das Doppelte größer werden.
The bread will become twice as big.

Frau Jung und August verlassen die Küche.
Mrs. Jung and August go out of the kitchen.
Das Brot fängt an, größer zu werden.
The bread begins to get bigger.

Eine Stunde später kommen Frau Jung und August zurück.
An hour later Mrs. Jung and August come back.

Das Brot ist übergelaufen!
The bread has overflowed!

Die Heizung ist mit Brot bedeckt.
The radiator is covered in bread.

Frau Jung sieht im Rezept nach.
Mrs. Jung looks at the recipe.

Es war zuviel Hefe in dem Brot.
There was too much yeast in the bread.

Das ist Augusts Schuld.
It's August's fault.

Frau Jung nimmt ein Stückchen von dem Brot.
Mrs. Jung takes a bit of bread.
Sie ißt es.
She eats it.

Das Brot ist gebacken.
The bread is cooked.
Ende gut, alles gut.
All's well that end's well.
August und Frau Jung haben ein köstliches Abendessen.
August and Mrs. Jung have a delicious supper.

Sie sitzen nicht am Tisch.
They don't sit at the table.

Sie essen von der Heizung!
They eat off the radiator!

Meine Familie
My family

Mein Onkel
My uncle
Er ist meines Vaters Bruder.
He is my father's brother.
Sie sind Zwillinge.
They are twins.

Ein anderer Onkel
Another uncle
Er ist der Mann
meiner liebsten Tante.
He's my favourite
aunt's husband.

Mein Patenonkel
My godfather

Meine Schwester
My sister
Sie schminkt sich gern.
She loves making herself up.

Meine liebste Tante
My favourite aunt

Mein Bruder
My brother

Meine Mutter
My mother
Sie versucht zu lächeln.
She is trying to smile.

Er ist neun Jahre alt, und er hat drei Meerschweinchen.
He is nine, and he has three guinea pigs.

Klaus ist der Hund meines Patenonkels.
Klaus is my godfather's dog.

Ich esse gern . . .
I like eating . . .

Ich esse gern Gemüse.
I like eating vegetables.

Ich mag besonders gerne:
I particularly like:

Erbsen
Peas

Mohrrüben
Carrots

Kartoffeln (besonders Pommes frites)
Potatoes (especially chips)

Salat
Lettuce

Gurken
Cucumbers

Rosenkohl
Brussels sprouts

Aber ich mag nicht:
But I don't like:

Spinat
Spinach

Zwiebeln
Onions

Ich esse gerne Obst.
I like eating fruit.

Mein liebstes Obst ist:
My favourite fruits are:

Ananas
Pineapples

Birnen
Pears

Pampelmusen (und Pampelmusensaft)
Grapefruit (and grapefruit juice)

Bananen
Bananas

Pfirsiche
Peaches

Melonen
Melons

Erdbeeren (und Erdbeereis)
Strawberries (and strawberry ice-cream)

Aprikosen (und besonders Aprikosenjogurt)
Apricots (particularly apricot yoghurt)

Pflaumen
Plums

Äpfel
Apples

Ich esse alle Früchte gern
—außer Zitronen.
I like eating all fruits—except lemons.

Ich mag Brot, mit einer Menge Butter und Marmelade.
I like bread, with lots of butter and jam.

Ich mag Kekse und Kuchen.
I like biscuits and cakes.

Ich mag Eier nicht gern.
I don't like eggs much.
Ich liebe Fleisch, besonders Hamburger.
I love meat, especially hamburgers.

Ich trinke gerne Coca-Cola oder Tee.
I like drinking Coca-Cola or tea.
Ich hasse Milch.
I hate milk.

Mein liebstes Gericht ist Spaghetti mit Tomatensauce, Käse und einem Würstchen.
My favourite dish is spaghetti with tomato sauce, cheese and a sausage.

Der Geburtstag
Peter the

Heinrich Groß bewundert Peter.
Henry Gross admires Peter.
Er möchte auch Astronaut sein.
He too wants to be an astronaut.

Peter schaut seinen Geburtstagskuchen an.
Peter is looking at his birthday cake.

Frau Jung
Mrs Jung
Sie hat den Geburtstagskuchen gestern gebacken.
She made the cake yesterday.
Sie ist sehr stolz auf ihn.
She is very proud of it.

Peters Geburtstagskuchen.
Peter's birthday cake
Er hat die Form des Mondes.
It is in the shape of the moon.

Kerzen
Candles

Limonade
Lemonade

Ein Glas
A glass

Tomatenbrote
Tomato sandwiches

Eine Tischdecke
A tablecloth

Eine Tasse
A cup

Ein Messer
A knife

Wer sitzt unter dem Tisch?
Who is under the table?

von Peter, dem Astronauten
astronaut's birthday

Frau Weiß
Mrs. Weiss
Sie ist eine Freundin von Peter.
She is a friend of Peter's.
Wenn er vom Mond zurückkommt, holt sie ihn immer mit ihrem Taxi ab.
When he comes back from the moon, she always collects him in her taxi.

August mag Geburtstage.
August loves birthdays.
Vor allem mag er Erdnüsse.
He particularly loves peanuts.

Erdnüsse
Peanuts

Ein Löffel
A spoon

Erdbeereis
Strawberry ice-cream
Heinrich Groß brachte zwei große Schüsseln Eis mit.
Henry Gross brought two large bowls of ice-cream.

Schinkenbrote
Ham sandwiches

Ein Schlips
A tie
Er ist ein Geschenk von Professor Julius.
It's a present from Professor Julius.
Wie viele Sterne kannst du sehen?
How many stars can you see?

Jeremias geht zum Rennen

Jeremy goes to the races

Jeremias friert und ist hungrig.
Jeremy is cold and hungry.

Er möchte sich eine Decke und etwas Käse kaufen.
He wants to buy himself a blanket and some cheese.

Aber er hat kein Geld.
But he has no money.

Aber er hat eine Menge Heidekraut.
But he has a lot of heather.
Er macht daraus viele kleine Sträußchen.
He makes it into lots of small sprigs.

Er geht zum Rennen.
He goes to the races.
An der Rennbahn sind viele Leute.
At the track there are a lot of people.

Jeremias verkauft einige Sträußchen Heidekraut.
Jeremy sells a few sprigs of heather.
Die Leute glauben, daß Heidekraut Glück bringt.
People think that heather is lucky.

Ein dicker Mann kauft vier Sträußchen.
A fat man buys four sprigs.

Sein Pferd wird im nächsten Rennen mitlaufen.
His horse is going to run in the next race.
Er braucht Glück.
He needs good luck.

Aber in zwei Stunden hat Jeremias nur zehn Sträußchen verkauft.
But in two hours Jeremy has sold only ten sprigs.

Plötzlich kommt der dicke Mann zurück.
Suddenly, the fat man comes back.
Sein Pferd hat gewonnen!
His horse has won!

Der dicke Mann ist sehr glücklich.
The fat man is very happy.
Er kauft das ganze Heidekraut von Jeremias.
He buys all Jeremy's heather.

Jeremias ist auch sehr glücklich.
Jeremy is very happy too.
Er hat genug Geld, um sich zwei Decken, etwas Käse, eine Schachtel Pralinen und eine Zigarre zu kaufen!
He has enough money to buy himself two blankets, some cheese, a box of chocolates and a cigar!

Seemöwen
Seagulls
Wolken
Clouds
Johannes schaut aus dem Fenster.
John is looking out of the window.
Er mag die Bewegungen des Luftkissenbootes.
He loves the movement of the hovercraft.
Er ist sehr glücklich.
He is very happy.
Es regnet.
It is raining.
Die Stewardeß
The hostess
Sie fliegt lieber mit dem Flugzeug.
She prefers travelling by plane.
Das Seewasser ist salzig.
The sea-water is salty.
Wellen
Waves

August auf dem Luftkissenboot
August in the hovercraft

Der Kapitän des Luftkissenbootes.
The captain of the hovercraft.

August schaut aus dem Fenster.
August is looking out of the window.
Welche Farbe hat Augusts Gesicht?
What colour is August's face?
Er ist seekrank.
He is feeling sea-sick.

Fiffi ist auch seekrank.
Fiffi is feeling sea-sick too.

Ein Fisch
A fish

Das Luftkissenboot
The hovercraft
Es berührt das Wasser nicht.
It does not touch the water.
Es schwebt auf einem Luftkissen.
It is on a cushion of air.

Wie viele Fische kannst du sehen?
How many fish can you see?

Ein Haus zu verkaufen
House for sale

Dieses Haus ist zu verkaufen.
This house is for sale.
Leute sehen es sich an.
People are looking at it.
Ist das Haus fertig?
Is the house finished?

Das Badezimmer
The bathroom
Wo ist die Badewanne?
Where is the bath?

Die Küche
The kitchen
Wo ist der Ausguß?
Where is the sink?

Der Kühlschrank
The refrigerator

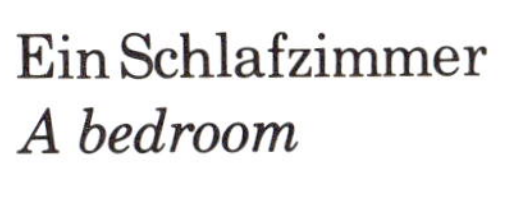

Ein Schlafzimmer
A bedroom

Wie viele Betten sind es?
How many beds are there?

Das Eßzimmer
The dining-room

Die Maurer und Maler sind hungrig.
The builders and painters are hungry.

Die Treppe
The staircase

Der Flur
The hall

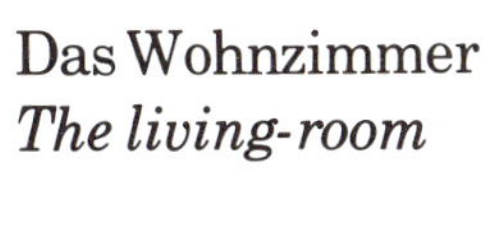

Das Wohnzimmer
The living-room

Ein Stuhl
A chair

Ein Sofa
A sofa

Ein Sessel
An armchair

Der Garten
The garden

Ein Schaufelbagger
A bulldozer

Im Büro
In an office

Ein Bild des Chefs
A painting of the boss.
Sieht es dem Chef ähnlich?
Does it look like the boss?

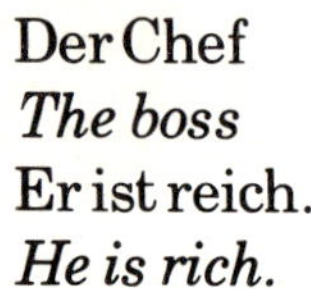

Der Chef
The boss
Er ist reich.
He is rich.
Er möchte noch reicher sein.
He wants to be even richer.

Eine Zigarre
A cigar

Die Chefsekretärin
The boss's secretary

Sie bedient beide Telefone.
She is answering both the telephones.

Sie spricht mit New York und Berlin zur gleichen Zeit.
She is talking to New York and to Berlin at the same time.

Aber sie kann kein Deutsch.
But she cannot speak German.

Darum spricht sie nicht viel mit Berlin.
So she is not saying much to Berlin.

Ein Kalender
A calendar
Teetassen und Kaffeetassen
Cups of tea and coffee
Der Fensterputzer
The window cleaner
Ein Ablageschrank
A filing cabinet
Briefe
Letters
Eine Schreibmaschine
A typewriter
Eine Stenotypistin
A shorthand-typist
Sie schreibt hundert Silben in einer Minute.
She writes a hundred words a minute.
Dieses Mädchen manikürt sich.
This girl is giving herself a manicure.

Große Gebäude
Big buildings

Eine Fabrik
A factory
Alle arbeiten.
Everybody is working.

Eine Schule
A school
Fast alle arbeiten.
Nearly everyone is working.

Ein Bürohaus
An office block

Ein Wohnblock
A block of flats
Was ist der Unterschied zwischen diesem Block und dem Bürohaus?
What differences are there between this block and the office block?

Ein Dom
A cathedral
Er ist sehr alt.
It is very old.

Eine Bücherei
A library
Dort gibt es überall Bücher.
There are books everywhere.

Ein Warenhaus
A department store
In diesem Geschäft kannst du alles kaufen, was du willst.
In this store you can buy everything you want.

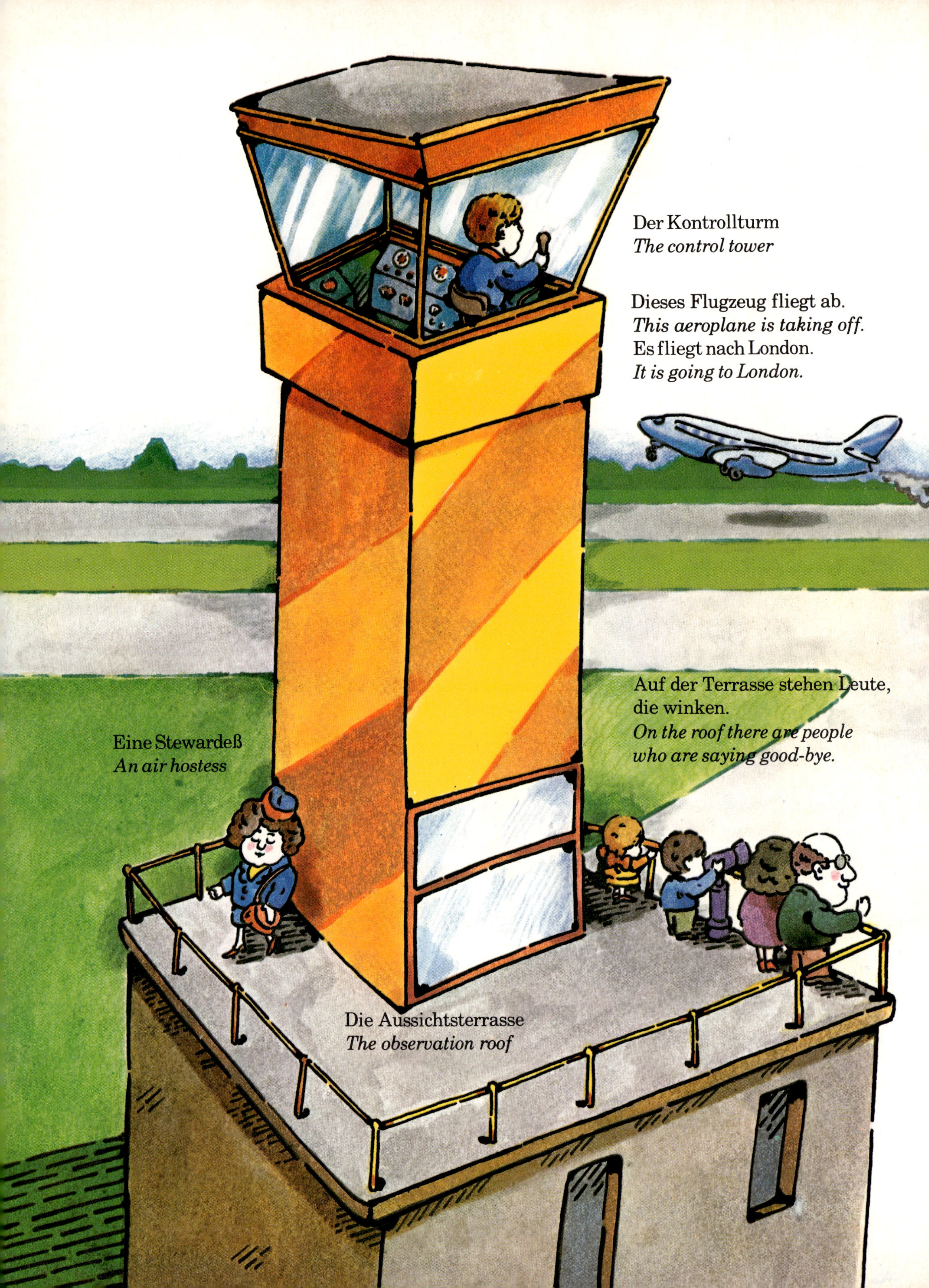
Der Kontrollturm
The control tower
Dieses Flugzeug fliegt ab.
This aeroplane is taking off.
Es fliegt nach London.
It is going to London.
Auf der Terrasse stehen Leute, die winken.
On the roof there are people who are saying good-bye.
Eine Stewardeß
An air hostess
Die Aussichtsterrasse
The observation roof

Auf dem Flughafen
At the airport

Dieses Flugzeug landet.
This aeroplane is landing.
Einer seiner Motoren hat ausgesetzt.
One of its engines has broken down.

Krankenwagen warten.
Ambulances are waiting.

Ein Flughafenbus
An airport bus
Er fährt zum Stadtterminal.
It goes to the town terminal.

Gepäck
Luggage

Ein Pilot
A pilot

Ein Düsenflugzeug
A jet plane

Ein Feuerwehrwagen
A fire engine

Die Diebe
The burglars

Es ist Winter.
It's winter.
August und Fiffi suchen einen warmen Ort, um dort die Nacht zu verbringen.
August and Fiffi are looking for a warm place to spend the night.

Auf der Straße sind aber auch zwei Diebe.
In the street there are also two burglars.
Die Diebe gehen zum Haus von Herrn und Frau Weiß.
The burglars go to Mr. and Mrs. Weiss' house.

Sie brechen das Türschloß auf.
They break the lock on the door.
Die Diebe füllen ihre Säcke.
The burglars fill their sacks.

Plötzlich hören sie ein Geräusch.
Suddenly they hear a noise.
Jette Weiß schlafwandelt.
Jane Weiss is walking in her sleep.

Herr und Frau Weiß wachen auf.
Mr. and Mrs. Weiss wake up.
Herr Weiß telefoniert mit der Polizei.
Mr. Weiss telephones the police.

Sie denken, sie sei ein Gespenst.
They think she is a ghost.
Sie laufen weg.
They run away.

Der Polizist führt die Diebe ab.
The policeman takes the burglars away.
Herr und Frau Weiß danken August.
Mr. and Mrs. Weiss thank August.

August und Fiffi sind da.
August and Fiffi are there.
Sie versuchen, sich aufzuwärmen.
They are trying to get warm.
August hält die Diebe fest und Fiffi bellt.
August grabs the burglars and Fiffi barks.

Sie geben ihm ein warmes und bequemes Bett.
They give him a warm and comfortable bed.
August und Fiffi sind sehr glücklich.
August and Fiffi are very happy.

Im Wachsfigurenkabinett

Johanna von Orleans
Joan of Arc
Sie ist Frankreichs Nationalheldin
She is the heroine of France.

Ein Attentäter
An assassin

Ein anderer Attentäter
Another assassin

August sieht sich einen Museumswärter an.
August is looking at a museum worker.
Er denkt, daß der Wärter aus Wachs ist.
He thinks the worker is made of wax.

Die beiden Attentäter schmieden einen Plan.
The two assassins are plotting.

Ein Politiker
A politician

Zwei Schlagersänger
Two pop stars

At the wax museum

Königin Elisabeth I. von England
Queen Elizabeth I of England
Sie trug oft Perlen im Haar.
She often wore pearls in her hair.

Muhammad Ali,
der Boxweltmeister
Muhammad Ali,
the boxing champion

Ein Entdecker des neunzehnten Jahrhunderts
A nineteenth-century explorer

Ein Fußballspieler
A footballer

Johannes sieht sich den Fußballspieler an.
John is looking at the footballer.
Er möchte Berufsfußballspieler werden.
He wants to be a professional footballer.

Indianer
Red Indians

Wie kommen sie von Ort zu Ort?
How do they get around?

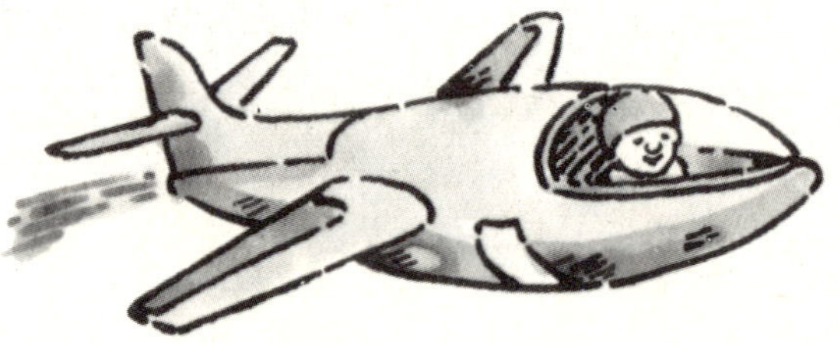

Der Pilot fliegt in seinem Düsenflugzeug.
The pilot flies in a jet plane.

Jeremias fährt in seinem Wohnwagen.
Jeremy gets around in his caravan.
Sein Pferd geht sehr langsam.
His horse goes very slowly.
Wenn es hungrig ist, bleibt das Pferd stehen.
When he's hungry, the horse stops.

Fiffi geht.
Fiffi walks.
Wenn er sehr müde ist, wird er von August getragen.
When he is very tired August carries him.

Peter fliegt mit seinem Raumschiff.
Peter gets around in a spacecraft.

Moritz fliegt.
Maurice flies.
Er fliegt sehr schnell.
He goes very fast.
Er hat nie Schwierigkeiten im Straßenverkehr.
He never has problems with the traffic.

August geht zu Fuß.
August gets around on foot.
Er geht nicht sehr schnell.
He doesn't go very quickly.

Frau Weiß fährt mit ihrem Taxi.
Mrs. Weiss gets around in her taxi.
Sie fährt gern schnell.
She likes going fast.
Wenn der Verkehr stockt, ist sie wütend.
When the traffic is bad she is furious.

Der Busfahrer fährt mit einem Bus.
The bus driver gets around in a bus.

Der Millionär fährt mit einer großen Jacht.
The millionaire gets around in a big yacht.

Fräulein Braun fährt nicht gern schnell.
Miss Braun doesn't like going fast.
Sie fährt mit ihrem Fahrrad.
She gets around on a bicycle.

Marianne Rund hat ein Paar Rollschuhe.
Marion Rund has got some roller skates.
Ihre weißen Mäuse laufen gern schnell.
Her white mice love going fast.

Und du?
And you?

Wie kommst du von Ort zu Ort?
How do you get around?

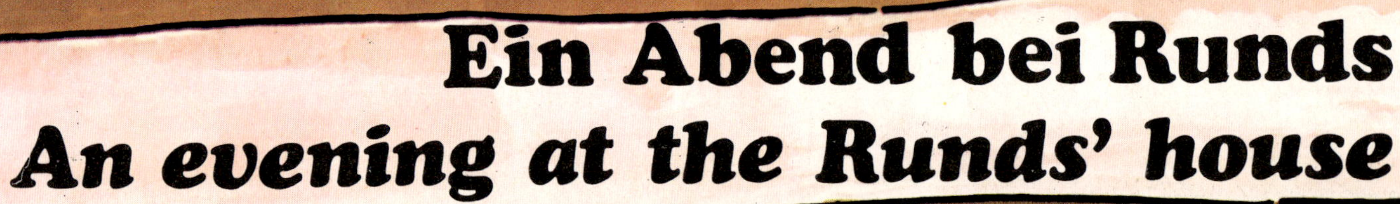

Ein Abend bei Runds
An evening at the Runds' house

Herr Rund sieht fern.
Mr. Rund is looking at the television.

Herrn Runds Hund
Mr. Rund's dog

Er mag Sportprogramme gern.
He loves sports programmes.

Gummistiefel
Rubber boots

Wie viele Paare sind es?
How many pairs are there?

Ein Lamm
A lamb

Es hat keine Mutter.
It has no mother.

Weißt du das?
Do you know?

Die Monate des Jahres	*The months of the year*
Januar	*January*
Februar	*February*
März	*March*
April	*April*
Mai	*May*
Juni	*June*
Juli	*July*
August	*August*
September	*September*
Oktober	*October*
November	*November*
Dezember	*December*

Die Tage der Woche	*The days of the week*
Montag	*Monday*
Dienstag	*Tuesday*
Mittwoch	*Wednesday*
Donnerstag	*Thursday*
Freitag	*Friday*
Sonnabend	*Saturday*
Sonntag	*Sunday*

Die Jahreszeiten	*The seasons of the year*
Frühling	*Spring*
Sommer	*Summer*
Herbst	*Autumn*
Winter	*Winter*

Der Kompaß	*The compass*
Norden	*North*
Süden	*South*
Osten	*East*
Westen	*West*

Auf Reisen	*Travelling*
Die Straße	*the road*
Eine Hauptstraße	*a main road*
Die Autobahn	*the motorway*
Durchfahrt verboten	*closed to traffic*
Anhalten verboten	*no parking*
Lastwagen	*lorries*
Rechts fahren	*keep right*
Weiter fahren!	*move along!*
Achtung!	*look out!*
Ein Strafzettel	*a (parking or other) ticket*
Ein Polizist	*a policeman*
Hilfe!	*help!*
Es tut mir leid	*I am sorry*
Entschuldigung!	*sorry*
Entschuldigen Sie bitte	*excuse me*

Die Kontinente	*The continents*
Afrika	*Africa*
Asien	*Asia*
Australasien	*Australasia*
Europa	*Europe*
Nordamerika	*North America*
Südamerika	*South America*

Einige Länder	*Some countries*
Australien	*Australia*
Österreich	*Austria*
Argentinien	*Argentina*
Belgien	*Belgium*
Kanada	*Canada*
die Kanalinseln	*The Channel Islands*
Dänemark	*Denmark*
England	*England*
Irland	*Eire (Ireland)*
Finnland	*Finland*
Frankreich	*France*
Deutschland	*Germany*
Griechenland	*Greece*
Holland	*Holland*
Ungarn	*Hungary*
Italian	*Italy*
Mexiko	*Mexico*
Luxembourg	*Luxemburg*
Nordirland	*Northern Ireland*
Norwegen	*Norway*
Neu Seeland	*New Zealand*
Polen	*Poland*
Portugal	*Portugal*
Russland	*Russia*
Schottland	*Scotland*
Südafrika	*South Africa*
Spanien	*Spain*
Schweden	*Sweden*
Schweiz	*Switzerland*
Türkei	*Turkey*
Die Vereinigten Staaten von Amerika	*United States of America*
Wales	*Wales*
Jugoslawien	*Yugoslavia*

Einige Farben	*Some colours*
rot	*red*
blau	*blue*
grün	*green*
gelb	*yellow*
weiß	*white*
schwarz	*black*
violett	*violet*
braun	*brown*
kastanienbraun	*maroon*
rosa	*pink*
orange	*orange*
dunkelrot	*dark red*

Einige Zahlen	*Some numbers*
eins	*one*
zwei	*two*
drei	*three*
vier	*four*
fünf	*five*
sechs	*six*
sieben	*seven*
acht	*eight*
neun	*nine*
zehn	*ten*
elf	*eleven*
zwölf	*twelve*
dreizehn	*thirteen*
vierzehn	*fourteen*
fünfzehn	*fifteen*
sechzehn	*sixteen*
siebzehn	*seventeen*
achtzehn	*eighteen*
neunzehn	*nineteen*
zwanzig	*twenty*
hundert	*a hundred*

A page for parents

I can read German is not intended to be a child's only source of German, but to be a supplement to other sources. For the child who knows no German it can be used in English, with occasional German words and phrases brought in as and when the parent feels the child can deal with them. In this way, the book can be used as a very gradual introduction to German. However, it will probably be more widely used by children who know a little German; and the following suggestions are given for such a child.

First of all, either the child reading the book, or the parent or friend, should know how to pronounce the German words in it. To get the greatest benefit the child should be helped with pronunciation (see page 8). Many of the words reappear several times in the book, and if they are pronounced wrongly the first time, will be thoroughly but incorrectly learned by the end of the book.

The section *Augusts Freunde* (pages 12 to 15) should be read first, as it introduces many characters who reappear throughout the book. After that, the sections can be read in any order as each is complete in itself. Children who know only very little German should start with the sections which have the smallest number of sentences, for example *Vom Hubschrauber aus* (page 32) and *Frühmorgens im Garten* (page 48). Usually the sections in full colour contain a greater number of isolated words than the sections in two colours, many of which use sentences to tell a story.

After reading a few sections with both the German and English visible, many children will enjoy going back to one section and testing their knowledge by covering up the English with a piece of paper, and seeing how much of the German they really know. The illustrations will help to show the meaning. The child should always study them when trying to find a meaning, rather than automatically refer to the English translation. If he works out the meaning for himself, and uses the translation only as a final check, he is far more likely to remember what he has learned. Throughout the book, occasional easy questions are asked, to which the reader should be encouraged to give answers in German.

Its author hopes that *I can read German* will entertain and teach at one and the same time.